Best Selling Series
CONSOLIDATION EXERCISES

PHOTOCOPIABLE
MASTERS

Level 3

Spelling Made

Consolidation Exercises For Spelling Made Easy
Level 3 Text Book

---

by
Violet Brand and Katy Brand

Fun with Phonics
Consolidation Exercises
for
Spelling Made Easy Level 3
First published in the United Kingdom in 2005
by Violet and Katy Brand

Copyright assigned to BrandBooks
(a division of G & M Brand Publications Ltd) Violet Brand and Katy Brand (2005)

ISBN 1-904421-172

All rights reserved. The copymasters contained in this publication are protected by international copyright laws. The copyright of all materials in the 'Spelling Made Easy' series remains the property of the publisher and the authors. The publisher hereby grants photocopying rights of this work for use with 'Spelling Made Easy' textbooks. Otherwise, no part of this book may be reproduced or translated in any form or by any means, electronic or mechanical, including recording or by any information storage or retrieval system without permission in writing from the publisher.

CONTENTS

Fun with Phonics Level 3

Introduction

	Exercises	page	Answers page
1.	Magic 'e' a-e, i-e, o-e, u-e	2,3	42
2.	Magic 'e' a-e, i-e, o-e, u-e	4,5	43
3.	Various Double Consonants 1 ur, tion	6,7	44
4.	Various Double Consonants 1 ur, tion	8,9	45
5.	Various Soft c, Double Consonants 2, . . . ful	10,11	46
6.	Various Soft c, Double Consonants 2, . . . ful	12,13	47
7.	Various ch (k), ly, or	14,15	48
8.	Various ch (k), ly, or	16,17	49
9.	Various Silent Letters 1 and 2, ough/eigh	18,19	50
10.	Various Silent Letters 1 and 2, ough/eigh	20,21	51
11.	Various Soft g, ar, ous, ary/able	22,23	52
12.	Various Soft g, ar, ous, ary/able	24,25	53
13.	Various le, er, y (i)	26,27	54
14.	Various le, er, y (i)	28,29	55
15.	Various sion, ie/ei, ent/ence	30,31	56
16.	Various sion, ie/ei, ent/ence	32,33	57
17.	Various al, y (i), ea (ē)	34,35	58

(Cont.)

Contents (Continued)

	Exercises	page	Answers page
18.	Various al, y (i), ea (ē)	36, 37	59
19.	Various our, ance/ant	38, 39	60
20.	Various our, ance/ant	40, 41	61

INTRODUCTION

BrandBooks is delighted to bring you Fun With Phonics, a series of consolidation exercises to perfectly complement the rest of Violet Brand's best-selling Spelling Made Easy series. Fun With Phonics comprises a set of four workbooks, colour-coded to match each of the existing textbooks and worksheet books.

Each Fun With Phonics book is fully photocopiable and designed to be used in conjunction with its corresponding textbook. Each book takes between two and five of the word families found in the textbook and provides four pages of interesting and stimulating exercises, including passages for reading aloud, reading comprehension tests, word searches, crosswords and much more.

Each series of exercises is based on a continuous story featuring Sam and Gus, the well-known characters from the textbooks. In many cases pupils will not recognise that they are being tested and that basic skills are being reinforced. Field tests have shown that pupils simply enjoy them. They are designed to put the fun into phonics!

The Spelling Made Easy series was conceived, written and published at a time when teaching reading and spelling though phonics was out of fashion in the UK, as were multi-sensory techniques.

After publication in 1984 the textbook series was quickly recognised as highly effective and it continues to be widely used and purchased by primary and special schools in the UK and their equivalents in other parts of the world where English is taught.

Violet Brand was awarded the MBE for services to literacy, and has always believed that literacy skills must be taught in a way that is both relevant and fun in order to become a tool for life.

"Spelling in isolation is not enough. The word building skills acquired must be integrated into literacy generally. For a few children this will happen automatically, but for others, tasks which will gently edge them along the path will be essential. Constant reinforcement will be necessary."

– Violet Brand MBE

1. Magic 'e'
'a-e', 'i-e', 'o-e', 'u-e'

Spelling Made Easy
Level 3 Textbook
Pages 6 – 13

1a Reading Exercise

The Dilapidated House: Part One

Sam and Gus have been great friends for many years. They like one another's company, they love to laugh and they have had many adventures together. One fine morning, Sam and Gus are sitting in a café. Sam is having a cup of coffee, and Gus is having his favourite drink – a large mug of hot chocolate with whipped cream. They each have a scone and jam to eat. They are reading separate newspapers and chatting happily. Sam is feeling a little tired because a noisy cat has kept him up all night. He yawns widely and takes a sip of his tea.

Suddenly, Gus sits up very straight. He seems excited about something he has seen in his paper. He shows Sam an advertisement on page nineteen. It gives details of an old, dilapidated house that is for sale. Gus wants to acquire the house and repair it, make it safe and turn it into a top hotel. He thinks it would be fun, and they could make a lot of money and retire! Sam is not so sure. He wants to take a good look at the house to see the damage. It has been disused for over twenty years and is likely to be beyond repair. They decide to go to the house immediately. Gus believes that he can definitely persuade Sam to buy the place . . .

1b Reading Comprehension

Answer the following questions on a separate sheet of paper.

1. Why are Sam and Gus friends?
2. What is Gus's favourite drink?
3. Why is Sam feeling tired?
4. What has Gus seen in his newspaper that makes him excited?
5. What does Gus want to do with the old house?

1c Wordsearch

There are 9 words from the story hidden in the box below. They go from left to right and top to bottom.

c	h	o	c	o	l	a	t	e	p
x	r	a	u	m	a	h	r	d	e
s	v	c	w	t	g	o	s	b	r
c	g	q	u	n	u	z	u	x	s
o	m	u	f	s	a	r	r	y	u
n	l	i	k	e	l	y	e	j	a
e	k	r	i	f	d	b	r	w	d
a	v	e	r	b	p	l	a	c	e
x	d	i	s	u	s	e	d	w	b
n	i	n	e	t	e	e	n	a	v

1d Find the Word

Take a red pen and carefully circle all the words in the story that use magic 'e'.

1e Creative Writing

On a separate sheet of paper, write a paragraph of 100 words describing a dilapidated old house.

2. Magic 'e'
   'a-e', 'i-e', 'o-e', 'u-e'

Spelling Made Easy
Level 3 Textbook
Pages 6 – 13

2a   Reading Exercise

The Dilapidated House: Part Two

Sam and Gus arrive at the huge gates of the dilapidated house. It is dark and dirty and seems to rise high above them. It has an air of loneliness about it and the west wall is badly eroded. Sam shivers as he feels a definite drop in temperature. Gus smiles bravely and pushes the gate. It creaks and whines as it swings open. They start to walk up the path. Sam notices the banks of weeds that slope away down to the road behind them. They reach the front door. Sam thinks they have made a mistake in coming to the house. He has a strange feeling about it all. Gus insists they have a look at the damage. He is thinking about how many people it could accommodate if it became a hotel.

Sam sees a picture on the wall of a sad, old man. He seems to be frowning at the two friends. A piece of paper flutters down the stairs and lands at Sam's feet. He picks it up and reads the message, 'From the wisdom of ages, I bring you this message. Stand back and admire, but do not acquire. This house has no hope, your mistake is to probe!' A soft wind blows through the hallway, rustling their clothes and hair. Sam and Gus look at each other and realise they must get out of the house as fast as they can. They turn and run down the path, pulling the gates shut.

2b Reading Comprehension

Answer the following questions on a separate sheet of paper.

1. Write a sentence to describe the house.
2. Why does Sam think they have made a mistake in coming to the house?
3. According to the story, what is Gus thinking about the house?
4. What is the note trying to communicate to Sam and Gus?
5. What do the two friends pull shut when they leave?

2c Wordsearch

There are 10 words from the story hidden in the box below. They go from left to right and top to bottom.

a	c	c	o	m	m	o	d	a	t	e
d	g	d	u	n	z	s	x	d	e	c
g	r	f	d	s	w	t	h	m	m	u
m	i	s	t	a	k	e	g	i	p	z
w	s	i	f	h	y	f	r	r	e	n
t	e	c	v	o	a	v	b	e	r	p
c	v	b	r	a	v	e	l	y	a	r
p	i	c	t	u	r	e	w	c	t	o
b	v	e	y	s	s	v	y	b	u	b
f	s	l	o	p	e	y	a	v	r	e
w	q	d	e	f	i	n	i	t	e	z

2d New Words

On a separate sheet of paper, write down 8 words from the 'a-e', 'i-e', 'o-e', 'u-e' word families. Try to think of 2 words for each family.

2e Drawing

On a separate sheet of paper, draw a picture of Sam and Gus in the old house then colour it in.

3. Various   Spelling Made Easy
   Double Consonants 1, 'ur', 'tion'   Level 3 Textbook
                                                    Pages 14 – 19

3a Reading Exercise

The Jewellery Burglar: Part One

It is a cold and foggy night. A couple called Adam and Cherry have sent Sam and Gus an invitation to come for dinner, and now the pair of friends are on their way to Adam and Cherry's home in the sleepy suburbs of London. Adam and Cherry sent Sam an email with directions to the house, but Sam has left the printout at home, and now he and Gus are lost. Sam can just remember the address, and he and Gus are walking around the area, trying to find a person to ask for help. A man creeps out of a bush by the side of the road, making Gus jump. The man had been hidden by the fog. Gus calls out to him, but he just looks round and then disappears into the night.

Sam is disappointed, but Gus has a strange feeling about the man. He paid close attention to the man's face and clothes. He mentions his odd feeling to Sam, and thinks they should pursue the man. Sam knows that they are late for Adam and Cherry, but he hears the urgency in his friend's voice. Gus has good instincts and a courage of conviction about his feelings, so Sam agrees to go after the man. They move quickly and quietly in the direction the strange man took. He seems to have headed back towards the station so the two excited friends retrace their steps.

3b Reading Comprehension

Answer the following questions on a separate sheet of paper.

1. Where is Adam and Cherry's house?
2. What was in the email Adam and Cherry sent to Sam?
3. What can Sam just about remember?
4. What does Gus suggest to Sam, as a result of his strange feeling?
5. Why does Sam agree to go after the man?

3c Wordsearch

There are 8 words from the story hidden in the box below. They go from left to right and top to bottom.

d	i	r	e	c	t	i	o	n	d
a	g	h	s	e	s	v	p	j	i
s	u	m	e	n	t	i	o	n	s
t	p	u	r	s	u	e	g	k	a
a	z	w	t	f	r	h	i	l	p
t	v	o	s	c	g	f	g	s	p
i	a	d	d	r	e	s	s	a	e
o	g	h	d	u	n	b	w	m	a
n	t	y	c	s	c	n	m	t	r
r	f	o	g	g	y	h	d	a	s

3d Find the Word

Take a red pen and carefully circle all the words in the story that have a double consonant or are from the 'ur' and 'tion' word families.

3e Creative Writing

On a separate sheet of paper, write a letter to the local police station describing the strange man and his behaviour, as detailed in the story. Add some ideas of your own.

4. Various   Spelling Made Easy
    Double Consonants 1, 'ur', 'tion'   Level 3 Textbook
                                                           Pages 14 – 19

4a   Reading Exercise

The Jewellery Burglar: Part Two

Gus and Sam reach the station but there is no sign of the strange man. Gus thinks he must have slipped down a side road. The fog is so thick now that the two men can barely see each other, let alone anyone else. Sam calls Adam on his mobile phone to let him know what is happening. Adam tells Sam to be careful as there has been a spate of burglaries in the area, and the gang may be lurking. Gus wonders if the man might be the burglar – if they catch him, they will be heroes!

Suddenly they hear a crash of broken glass and a scream. They turn and run in the direction of the sound. They leap over a turnstile and into a quiet street. Sam can see the broken window a little further down the road, and they slow down. They want to creep up and surprise the burglar in action. They use the foggy night to hide themselves, and make their way up to the house. Crouching under the window, they can hear a rough male voice asking a woman to fetch her jewellery. Gus and Sam leap into action. They hurtle through the window. Gus pushes the burglar to the floor and Sam grabs the dagger in his hand. He is very surprised by the interruption. Gus sees that it is the strange man! The police arrive and take the man away. 'Come on,' says Gus. 'Let's go for our dinner – all this work has made me hungry!'

4b Reading Comprehension

Answer the following questions on a separate sheet of paper.

1. Why does Adam tell Sam to be careful?
2. What makes the crash that Sam and Gus hear?
3. Why do Sam and Gus want to creep up to the house?
4. What does Sam grab out of the burglar's hand?
5. What is the burglar surprised by?

4c Wordsearch

There are 9 words from the story hidden in the box below. They go from left to right and top to bottom.

h	a	p	p	e	n	i	n	g	d
a	d	i	r	e	c	t	i	o	n
f	g	s	r	u	d	s	t	m	w
o	b	u	r	g	l	a	r	f	a
j	d	e	y	h	u	k	p	o	c
d	a	g	g	e	r	j	l	g	t
c	f	v	b	n	k	t	y	g	i
s	u	r	p	r	i	s	e	y	o
w	q	f	t	g	n	g	m	b	n
f	g	s	r	y	g	l	a	s	s

4d New Words

On a separate sheet of paper, write down 6 words using double consonants and from the 'ur' and 'tion' word families. Try to think of 2 words for each family.

4e Drawing

On a separate sheet of paper, draw a picture of Sam and Gus surprising the burglar in the lady's house and colour it in.

5. **Various**   **Spelling Made Easy**
    Soft c, Double Consonants 2, . . . ful   Level 3 Textbook
                                                             Pages 20 – 25

5a Reading Exercise

A Trip to the Circus: Part One

It is a beautiful sunny morning. Sam wakes up very excited. He is going on a trip to the circus. Sam loves the circus. He thinks it is brilliant. He really loves the clowns when they throw buckets of water over each other. Even when he is annoyed about something, he will recollect the time he saw clowns when he was a young boy and have a good laugh. Sam's best friend Gus is going to the circus too. He also thinks clowns are wonderful! Sam has his breakfast and gets dressed. He drives to Gus's little house and beeps the horn. Gus runs out and climbs into the passenger seat. Sam puts his foot on the accelerator and they are on their way!

The circus starts at three o'clock. It is already half past two and they are running late. They get to the tunnel that runs under the river. The traffic is terrible. There has been an accident inside the tunnel. Sam is a skilful driver, but there is nothing he can do. They are stuck. Sam puts the radio on nice and loud. Gus's favourite song is playing and they both sing along. The people in the other cars see that Sam and Gus are having a good time, and they put their own radios on. The sun is shining and it is a lovely day. Sam and Gus are late for the circus but they are not too annoyed. They will make it in time to see the clowns.

5b Reading Comprehension

Answer the following questions on a separate sheet of paper.

1. What does Sam wake up feeling excited about?
2. How does Sam deal with feeling annoyed?
3. What does Gus think about clowns?
4. What is the traffic like, and why?
5. What sort of driver is Sam?

5c Wordsearch

There are 8 words from the story hidden in the box below. They go from right to left and top to bottom.

g	h	r	u	n	n	i	n	g	u	f
a	c	c	e	l	e	r	a	t	o	r
n	e	g	s	v	s	e	a	r	b	m
n	s	w	c	r	t	c	v	g	h	k
o	k	j	i	d	s	o	t	s	q	o
y	i	b	r	i	l	l	i	a	n	t
e	l	g	c	b	x	l	w	q	i	m
d	f	i	u	q	w	e	b	f	x	o
s	u	v	s	b	u	c	y	o	e	i
z	l	f	g	s	r	t	i	f	o	f
a	w	o	n	d	e	r	f	u	l	g

5d Find the Word

Take a red pen and carefully circle all the words in the story that have a double consonant, a soft c or are from the 'ful' word family.

5e Creative Writing

On a separate sheet of paper, write a paragraph of 100 words to describe a circus.

6.   **Various**   Spelling Made Easy
      Soft c, Double Consonants 2, . . . ful   Level 3 Textbook
                                                                          Pages 20 – 25

6a   Reading Exercise

A Trip to the Circus: Part Two

Sam and Gus are enjoying themselves listening to music. They almost forget that they are stuck in a traffic jam. They are not bitter. There is no point in getting aggressive as there is nothing they can do but wait. They just have to accept the situation. They are very grateful for the radio as it has kept them entertained. Suddenly, at ten to three the accident is cleared and the traffic starts to move. They are hopeful that they will not be late.

Sam and Gus finally arrive at the circus at quarter past three. It is in a big field away from the main road. They find the access road to the car park and drive up to an empty space. They can barely contain their excitement as they run to the Big Top. It is a huge tent with yellow and red stripes. It has flags on top and a lot of noise is coming from inside. Gus thinks the Big Top is beautiful. They are in a hurry so they run through the first entrance they can see. Suddenly they stop stock still. All around them are laughing faces and ponies and people in bright costumes. They have run through the wrong entrance and into the middle of the ring! The crowd think that Sam and Gus are clowns. Sam grabs a bucket and throws it over Gus. The crowd go crazy and the real clowns are all laughing too. The two friends run out to dry off. They hug each other, grinning and smiling. Their dream to be clowns has come true.

6b Reading Comprehension

Answer the following questions on a separate sheet of paper.

1. How do Sam and Gus feel about the traffic jam?
2. What is cleared from the tunnel, allowing the traffic to move?
3. What colour is the Big Top?
4. What does Gus think of the Big Top?
5. How do Sam and Gus end up in the middle of the circus ring?

6c Wordsearch

There are 8 words from the story hidden in the box below. They go from left to right and top to bottom.

d	h	o	p	e	f	u	l	a	w
v	b	a	b	f	d	s	n	c	m
h	j	i	i	g	h	m	k	c	s
g	r	a	t	e	f	u	l	e	p
f	t	n	t	a	s	d	k	s	a
e	r	t	e	s	c	a	h	s	c
a	g	g	r	e	s	s	i	v	e
f	a	y	b	n	u	j	f	k	l
z	t	r	a	f	f	i	c	x	c
w	t	y	x	a	c	c	e	p	t

6d New Words

On a separate sheet of paper, write down 6 words that use a double consonant, a soft 'c' or are from the 'ful' family. Try to think of 2 words for each family.

6e Drawing

On a separate sheet of paper, draw a picture of a clown then colour it in.

7. Various
    'ch' (k), 'ly', 'or'

Spelling Made Easy
Level 3 Textbook
Pages 26 – 31

7a Reading Exercise

The Christmas Choir: Part One

It is Christmas and Sam wants to decorate his house. Gus comes over to help out. Sam gets a box of assorted decorations down from the attic and the two friends begin immediately. It takes around three hours but when they have finished they feel really pleased with their work. They have decorated the house beautifully. Now it's really starting to feel like Christmas!

Gus shows Sam a clipping from the local newspaper. It is for a Christmas choir at the local school hall. Anybody can join, no matter how musical they are. There will be one rehearsal and then there will be a concert in the evening. It sounds very exciting! Sam and Gus decide to go along and join in. Sam is particularly looking forward to the concert as he has never been involved in a big performance before. Gus is excited too, but he is also very nervous about singing in public. He feels a knot in his stomach. Gus is a brave man and he does not like feeling nervous about things. He wants to confront his nerves and really get stuck in! Gus is no ordinary man and that is why Sam likes him so much. They change their clothes – they need to be smart for the performance. Gus and Sam have a last look at the beautifully decorated house and head off to the school.

7b Reading Comprehension

Answer the following questions on a separate sheet of paper.

1. What does Sam get down from the attic, and why?
2. What is Gus's newspaper clipping about?
3. Why is Sam looking forward to the concert?
4. According to the story, why does Sam like Gus so much?
5. Where is the concert rehearsal being held?

7c Wordsearch

There are 8 words from the story hidden in the box below. They go from left to right and top to bottom.

w	a	f	c	z	a	g	j	u	o
x	s	c	h	o	o	l	o	s	r
v	s	b	u	i	d	s	t	t	d
i	o	v	c	h	o	i	r	o	i
d	r	v	f	s	a	t	h	m	n
o	t	a	s	c	g	d	p	a	a
d	e	c	o	r	a	t	e	c	r
g	d	w	h	k	o	p	m	h	y
f	g	r	e	a	l	l	y	j	i
c	h	r	i	s	t	m	a	s	l

7d Find the Word

Take a red pen and carefully circle all the words in the story that are from the 'ch', 'ly' and 'or' word families.

7e Creative Writing

On a separate sheet of paper, write a paragraph of 100 words to describe a house decorated for Christmas.

8. **Various**
    'ch' (k), 'ly', 'or'

Spelling Made Easy
Level 3 Textbook
Pages 26 – 31

8a Reading Exercise

The Christmas Choir: Part Two

Sam and Gus arrive at the school hall for the choir practice. It is chaos! There are people chattering excitedly. The choir is run by a couple called Christine and Christopher. They are trying unsuccessfully to get all the people to talk a little more quietly whilst they organise the rehearsal. Sam and Gus take their seats and look around. There are more people than they had expected. There is an orchestra and an organ player too. Gus has never seen an orchestra before. It is very impressive!

Christine and Christopher finally get control of the noisy crowd. They are not angry – it is Christmas after all! The orchestra take their seats and pick up their instruments. The organist sits at his organ. They rehearse carols and songs all afternoon and finally Christine and Christopher are happy with the results. The evening's performance is important. The mayor is the sponsor of the show and there will be lots of junior and senior members of the local community watching. As the choir and orchestra file in, Gus sees the audience waiting. He feels butterflies in his stomach. But as the organ sounds the first chord, Gus feels his nerves evaporate. The music makes an echo around the huge hall and seems to fill the hearts of everyone in the room. From the chaos of the afternoon, Christine and Christopher have successfully made a wonderful Christmas concert.

8b Reading Comprehension

Answer the following questions on a separate sheet of paper.

1. Who runs the choir?
2. What are the couple trying to do when Sam and Gus arrive, and why?
3. What has Gus never seen before?
4. Who is the sponsor of the show, and who will be watching with him?
5. When does Gus feel his nerves evaporate?

8c Wordsearch

There are 8 words from the story hidden in the box below. They go from left to right and top to bottom.

s	p	o	n	s	o	r	e	g	j
o	d	f	r	a	e	f	c	u	o
r	h	k	l	s	t	x	h	b	r
g	t	y	s	a	j	k	o	n	c
a	m	o	r	g	a	n	g	w	h
n	d	s	r	y	s	b	j	d	e
i	u	q	u	i	e	t	l	y	s
s	f	g	s	r	a	z	y	w	t
e	m	k	d	c	h	o	r	d	r
e	x	c	i	t	e	d	l	y	a

8d New Words

On a separate sheet of paper, write down 6 words from the 'ch', 'ly' and 'or' word families. Try to think of 2 words for each family.

8e Drawing

On a separate sheet of paper draw a picture of a mayor then colour it in.

9. Various
Silent Letters 1 and 2, 'ough/eigh'

Spelling Made Easy
Level 3 Textbook
Pages 32 – 37

9a Reading Exercise

The Mad Scientist: Part One

Sam is having some building work done on his house and garden to improve the scenery. He goes into the garden to gather up his collection of gnomes. Sam has a great collection of gnomes and he loves them all. There ought to be eight gnomes, but today, Sam can only count seven. One of his gnomes is missing! Sam cannot think what has happened. He calls his best friend Gus. Gus does not know either. He can give Sam no answer. Sam is upset. He makes a thorough search of the garden, trying to find his eighth gnome. He kneels down and looks in all the nooks and crannies. He feels a knot in his stomach as he realises that the gnome is missing.

Sam feels awful so he asks Gus to come over. Gus arrives with a sign he has found on his way over. It says, 'SCIENTIFIC EXPERIMENT! I can make your garden gnomes come to life! Bring me the gnomes and I will show you how...Professor Alan Fluggle, 3a Windmill Lane.' Sam realises with a jolt that Professor Alan Fluggle is his neighbour. Gus tells Sam that he has had a brilliant idea. He thinks they should take one of Sam's remaining gnomes to Professor Fluggle, and when he comes to life Sam can ask him what happened to the missing gnome. Sam listens to Gus's idea. Although he feels it is a little odd, he cannot see what else to do. Sam chooses a clever looking gnome and they set off.

9b Reading Comprehension

Answer the following questions on a separate sheet of paper.

1. What is happening to Sam's house?
2. How many gnomes ought Sam to have?
3. What does Sam feel in his stomach?
4. What kind of experiment does the sign say the professor is carrying out?
5. Professor Fluggle lives close to Sam, so this makes him Sam's _____.

9c Wordsearch

There are 8 words from the story hidden in the box below. They go from left to right and top to bottom.

w	b	u	i	l	d	i	n	g	e
r	t	y	x	b	g	h	a	u	s
s	c	i	e	n	t	i	f	i	c
r	t	y	v	s	h	u	p	n	e
m	i	p	o	g	d	w	o	s	n
e	s	a	n	s	w	e	r	i	e
i	b	v	f	m	j	u	l	g	r
g	a	k	n	e	e	l	s	n	y
h	e	s	f	s	v	g	j	k	u
t	h	o	r	o	u	g	h	o	i

9d Find the Word

Take a red pen and carefully circle all the words in the story that use a silent letter, or are from the 'eigh' or 'ough' word families.

9e Creative Writing

On a separate sheet of paper, write a paragraph of 100 words to describe your garden, or the garden of someone you know.

10. Various
Silent Letters 1 and 2, 'ough/eigh'

Spelling Made Easy
Level 3 Textbook
Pages 32 – 37

10a Reading Exercise

The Mad Scientist: Part Two

Sam and Gus arrive at 3a Windmill Lane. It has a wooden sign outside that reads 'Professor Alan Fluggle, Mad Scientist and Gnome Lover.' There is a gnarled old tree next to the front door. Sam lifts the brass knocker on the door and knocks it twice. There is no answer so he knocks again. Sam thinks they should just go inside, but Gus feels they ought not to. Sam looks at his gnome and makes up his mind. He unfastens the latch and twists the door knob. Sam calls out and Gus makes a loud whistle. The house is a bit of an old wreck, but has a friendly feeling about it.

Sam and Gus climb the stairs. At the top is an amazing scene. A little old man is rushing around, placing little tubes on a big machine. On a tiny chair in the middle of the machine sits Sam's missing gnome. The little old man suddenly sees Sam and Gus, and stops still. He introduces himself as Professor Alan Fluggle and asks what they want. Sam tells Professor Alan that he seems to have his gnome. The mad scientist looks guilty and coughs. He offers Sam a biscuit and explains that he needed a gnome to start his experiment. He saw Sam's collection and hoped that he would not miss one. He was going to put the gnome back as soon as he had made him come to life. Sam listens, and then smiles. As Sam says he will collect his gnome in one week, he sees the little statue give a cheeky wink.

10b Reading Comprehension

Answer the following questions on a separate sheet of paper.

1. What does the wooden sign outside the professor's house say?
2. How does the story describe the tree in his garden?
3. What does Sam do to the latch on the door?
4. How does the professor look when Sam tells him he has the gnome?
5. What does the professor offer Sam?

10c Wordsearch

There are 8 words from the story hidden in the box below. They go from left to right and top to bottom.

w	r	c	o	u	g	h	s	o	g
d	f	g	t	y	u	c	z	s	n
f	j	o	r	v	s	a	w	m	o
k	n	o	c	k	e	r	o	w	m
e	t	u	b	s	g	z	u	t	e
w	n	s	c	e	n	e	g	a	d
r	f	h	y	u	s	n	h	m	l
e	b	i	s	c	u	i	t	w	t
c	c	v	b	s	q	f	k	l	g
k	j	k	g	u	i	l	t	y	u

10d New Words

On a separate sheet of paper, write down 6 words from the story that use a silent letter, or are from the 'eigh' or 'ough' word families. Try to think of 2 words for each family.

10e Drawing

On a separate sheet of paper, draw a picture of Professor Alan Fluggle and colour it in.

11. Various   **Spelling Made Easy**
      'Soft g', 'ar', 'ous', 'ary/able'   **Level 3 Textbook**
                                                                           Pages 38 – 45

11a Reading Exercise

Sam Gets Fit: Part One

Sam is famous throughout his village for his terrible eating habits. He eats lots of fatty foods because he thinks they taste good. He also does very little exercise. As a result Sam is very unfit. His friend Gus is the exact opposite. Gus loves to eat fruit and vegetables and he goes to the gym three times a week. Gus always has lots of energy. He loves to work in his garden. He has an apple orchard at the back of his garden and he picks the apples off the trees and eats them. Gus is very knowledgeable about healthy food and getting fit. Gus believes Sam is doing himself some damage by eating so badly.

One day, Sam and Gus are having lunch in Sam's favourite restaurant. Sam leans forward to eat a plate of chips and one of the buttons on his cardigan pops off. It hits an old lady in the face, which startles her. Sam ignores the button and orders a bowl of crumble with extra custard for pudding. Gus does not order any pudding. Sam licks his bowl clean and does a big burp. Sam's belly looks huge. Gus frowns – he feels the time is right to tell Sam that he is concerned about his lifestyle. He thinks a change is necessary. It could be awkward, so Gus knows he must be sensitive. Gus feels a bit nervous as he doesn't want to get into an argument with Sam.

11b Reading Comprehension

Answer the following questions on a separate sheet of paper.

1. What does Gus love to eat?
2. What does Gus have in the back of his garden?
3. What does Gus believe that Sam is doing by eating badly?
4. What does Sam order with his crumble?
5. How does Gus feel about getting into an argument with Sam?

11c Wordsearch

There are 8 words from the story hidden in the box below. They go from left to right and top to bottom.

v	e	g	e	t	a	b	l	e	s
o	f	f	g	t	y	u	n	m	f
c	d	a	n	e	r	v	o	u	s
a	a	m	g	y	m	h	j	k	d
r	m	o	h	u	p	c	z	s	w
d	a	u	r	t	c	n	z	x	f
i	g	s	f	o	r	w	a	r	d
g	e	g	j	i	p	v	z	s	w
a	m	n	c	d	j	u	s	w	a
n	e	c	e	s	s	a	r	y	o

11d Find the Word

Take a red pen and carefully circle all the words in the story that are from the 'soft g', 'ar', 'ous' and 'ary' or 'able' word families.

11e Creative Writing

On a separate sheet of paper write a healthy eating plan for one day.

12. Various   **Spelling Made Easy**
'Soft g', 'ar', 'ous', 'ary/able'   **Level 3 Textbook**
                                               Pages 38 – 45

12a Reading Exercise

Sam Gets Fit: Part Two

Sam and Gus have just finished their lunch. Sam has overeaten again and he tells Gus he feels very ill. Gus asks Sam to imagine how he would be feeling if he had eaten a healthier meal. Sam agrees he would now be feeling better. Sam looks at his huge belly. He is envious of Gus's slim build. He wishes he could fit into the trousers he wore as a young man. Sam's trouble is that he is very generous in spirit, both to other people and himself! This leads to him being a bit too generous with his food portions too! Gus offers to help. It is now January. Gus tells Sam that by the end of February he will have lost a stone.

Gus begins teaching Sam about eating properly. He shows him how to cook vegetables so that they taste good. They go on a trip to the local library to find some cookery books and read about the importance of exercising. Sam joins a gym. He is shown round by a friendly manager called George. He eats toast with marmalade and margarine for breakfast, instead of a fry-up. He eats lots of fresh fruit and low-fat food. He is very conscientious about his new lifestyle. He finds his trousers more spacious. At the end of February he weighs himself. He has lost a stone. Gus and Sam are delighted! Gus takes Sam to a department store to buy a new cardigan as a reward for all his hard work.

12b Reading Comprehension

Answer the following questions on a separate sheet of paper.

1. According to the story, what does Sam wish?
2. What month is it in the story?
3. What food group does Gus teach Sam how to cook?
4. What does Sam have on his toast?
5. What does Sam get as a reward for his hard work?

12c Wordsearch

There are 8 words from the story hidden in the box below. They go from right to left and top to bottom.

d	e	p	a	r	t	m	e	n	t
o	h	a	r	d	f	a	h	d	z
w	r	t	y	v	x	n	o	p	a
b	h	g	t	z	w	a	m	k	z
j	u	k	i	m	a	g	i	n	e
w	g	b	h	j	l	e	m	w	z
f	e	b	r	u	a	r	y	o	p
d	g	u	b	z	v	f	o	i	z
d	t	s	p	a	c	i	o	u	s
m	a	r	g	a	r	i	n	e	m

12d New Words

On a separate sheet of paper, write down 6 words from the story that use a silent letter, or are from the 'eigh' or 'ough' word families. Try to think of 2 words for each family.

12e Drawing

Divide a separate sheet of paper into two halves. On one side, draw a picture of fat Sam. On the other half, draw a picture of slim Sam. Colour in both of them.

13. Various
  'le', 'er', 'y' (i)

Spelling Made Easy
Level 3 Textbook
Pages 46 – 51

13a Reading Exercise

A Wonderful Holiday: Part One

Sam and Gus are fed up with the bad weather in the village. It is cold, rainy and generally miserable. Sam is desperate to see some sunshine. He and his friend Gus decide to go on holiday. They log on to the internet to find a last minute deal. Gus loves the Mediterranean and wants to go to Italy, but Sam finds a cheap holiday to Egypt. Neither Sam nor Gus has ever been to Africa, but Sam's uncle has. Sam manages to persuade Gus to take the deal to Egypt. They enter their credit card details, click the button and the holiday is booked. In less than a week, they will be on an aeroplane to Egypt and sunny weather. It is all very exciting!

It is the night before the holiday. Sam and Gus have to get up very early next morning to catch the plane. Gus stays over at Sam's house. They both get into their pyjamas at half past eight and sit in their separate bedrooms waiting. They are too excited to sleep. Sam is thinking about the Pyramids. He knows they will be incredible and he cannot wait to see them. Gus is dreaming about mysterious crypts that he can explore. They both hope that the temperature will be high. They drift into a light sleep and dream of the old Kings and Queens of Egypt, the sandy desert and camel rides. Suddenly the alarm clock goes off. Sam and Gus jump up and throw on their travelling clothes. They grab their suitcases, jump into Sam's car and head to the airport.

13b Reading Comprehension

Answer the following questions on a separate sheet of paper.

1. How is the weather in the village described in the story?
2. Where is Gus's first choice for a holiday, and why?
3. Where do Sam and Gus decide to go in the end?
4. What two things do Sam and Gus do at half past eight on the night before their holiday?
5. What does Gus dream about?

13c Wordsearch

There are 8 words from the story hidden in the box below. They go from right to left and top to bottom.

p	y	p	y	r	a	m	i	d	s
y	g	h	s	e	y	v	u	e	p
j	a	c	r	y	p	t	y	s	u
a	b	m	w	e	t	z	g	p	n
m	i	s	e	r	a	b	l	e	c
a	y	u	c	s	g	j	s	r	l
s	p	i	c	s	z	s	a	a	e
y	d	e	s	e	r	t	j	t	z
x	f	t	b	k	s	w	d	e	l
i	n	c	r	e	d	i	b	l	e

13d Find the Word

Take a red pen and carefully circle all the words in the story that are from the 'le', 'er' and 'y' word families.

13e Creative Writing

On a separate sheet of paper, write a paragraph of 100 words to describe the best holiday you have ever had.

14. Various
   'le', 'er', 'y' (i)

Spelling Made Easy
Level 3 Textbook
Pages 46 – 51

14a Reading Exercise

A Wonderful Holiday: Part Two

Sam and Gus fall asleep on the plane. When they wake up five hours later, they are in Egypt. It is hot and dusty. Sam checks the temperature on the thermometer in their hotel – it is 30° centigrade! This is very hot indeed! Sam and Gus are very sweaty as they unpack their clothes. They put all their shirts and trousers in the drawers provided and head out to the pool to cool off. The sun is fiery in the sky and it is impossible to exaggerate how hot it is. Sam and Gus dive into the water and splash around happily.

Later that afternoon they visit an old monastery. It is a bit creepy as it is over three thousand years old. Gus finds a crypt exactly like the one he dreamed about. Their guide tells them of a horrible murder once committed in the monastery and Gus shivers. Next they take a trip to the Pyramids. They are even more amazing than Sam had imagined. They are so old, Sam thinks they must be a miracle! They are surrounded in mystery as nobody knows exactly how they were built. Sam and Gus scramble up the sandy dunes around the biggest pyramid and find a man selling camel rides. Sam whispers to his camel that he thinks the Pyramids would be a great place to work – he is jealous of the camel! Gus and Sam get off their camels and grab a loose pebble from the ground as a souvenir. It is a wonderful holiday!

14b Reading Comprehension

Answer the following questions on a separate sheet of paper.

1. What does Sam check the temperature on?
2. Where do Sam and Gus put all their clothes when they unpack?
3. Where does the story tell us a horrible murder was committed?
4. Where does Sam think would be a great place to work?
5. What do Sam and Gus take as a souvenir?

14c Wordsearch

There are 8 words from the story hidden in the box below. They go from left to right and top to bottom.

h	f	h	t	j	c	a	e	y	j	l
o	i	m	p	o	s	s	i	b	l	e
r	b	n	d	r	s	a	e	y	j	k
r	x	m	y	s	t	e	r	y	c	f
i	v	j	l	u	i	t	v	d	l	i
b	o	s	c	r	a	m	b	l	e	e
l	f	d	r	s	g	n	m	c	s	r
e	r	y	y	j	k	d	q	o	p	y
t	e	m	p	e	r	a	t	u	r	e
b	v	z	t	w	e	g	y	k	g	d
m	o	n	a	s	t	e	r	y	a	f

14d New Words

On a separate sheet of paper, write down 6 words from the 'le', 'er' and 'y' word families. Try to think of 2 words for each family.

14e Drawing

On a separate sheet of paper, draw a picture of Sam riding a camel next to the Pyramids then colour it in.

15. Various   **Spelling Made Easy**
     'sion', 'ie/ei', 'ent/ence'   **Level 3 Textbook**
                                                              Pages 52 – 57

15a   Reading Exercise

A Trip to Parliament: Part One

Sam is watching television when he sees an interesting announcement. There is an invitation to all the residents of his village to visit the Houses of Parliament. Sam thinks he would like an excursion to London and so he calls up his best friend Gus. Gus has seen the announcement too, and thinks it is a great idea. Sam would like to invite his niece Wendy. She is ten years old and has never been to London or the Houses of Parliament before. Wendy asks her mother for permission to go. She receives permission and they make a decision to go the very next day.

The next morning Sam, Gus and Sam's niece Wendy meet at nine o'clock to catch the train to London. Wendy is a very intelligent and obedient girl, and so Sam knows they will all have a great day. To give a sense of occasion, Wendy's mother has packed a very expensive picnic, using the very best ingredients money can buy. They are all looking forward to eating it at lunchtime! The train is about to arrive at King's Cross station. Wendy lets out a piercing shriek of excitement. She cannot wait to get off the train. She is looking forward to seeing the green benches in the House of Commons and the red benches in the House of Lords. She is also excited about going on the London Eye and being high above the capital city. It will be a great experience.

15b Reading Comprehension

Answer the following questions on a separate sheet of paper.

1. What does Sam see on television?
2. What relation is Wendy to Sam?
3. What does Wendy have to ask her mother for before she can go to London?
4. Why has Wendy's mother packed an expensive picnic?
5. What does Wendy do when their train is about to arrive at the station?

15c Wordsearch

There are 8 words from the story hidden in the box below. They go from left to right and top to bottom.

i	l	o	c	c	a	s	i	o	n	h
n	g	d	s	h	r	i	e	k	a	d
t	r	e	s	i	d	e	n	t	s	i
e	e	g	j	k	l	n	x	z	a	l
l	c	e	d	e	c	i	s	i	o	n
l	e	f	b	m	s	e	w	t	s	z
i	i	b	h	k	d	c	t	y	z	w
g	v	e	w	q	z	e	b	k	c	z
e	e	m	l	k	v	u	o	f	g	p
n	s	e	x	c	u	r	s	i	o	n
t	r	t	z	a	m	p	w	q	r	u

15d Find the Word

Take a red pen and carefully circle all the words in the story that are from the 'sion', 'ie/ei' and 'ent/ence' word families.

15e Creative Writing

On a separate sheet of paper write a paragraph of 100 words about your local MP.

16. Various
'sion', 'ie/ei', 'ent/ence'

Spelling Made Easy
Level 3 Textbook
Pages 52 – 57

16a Reading Exercise

A Trip to Parliament: Part Two

The train finally pulls into King's Cross station. Everybody gets off, and in the confusion, Gus and Sam lose sight of Wendy, Sam's ten-year-old niece. They call and shout down the platform, but they cannot see her. They get very worried and run around the station calling her name. Suddenly the whole excursion seems like a very bad idea. In spite of Wendy's intelligence and obedience, she has got lost and London is a big place. Sam wipes his brow with a handkerchief. Suddenly he hears a small voice behind him, calling, 'Uncle Sam! Uncle Sam!' He turns round and sees Wendy running towards him. He cannot believe it. He feels great relief and gives her a big hug.

Sam, Gus and Wendy get on the bus to Westminster. They get off the bus over the road from the Houses of Parliament. They are quite magnificent. There is a procession going on outside. Wendy asks a priest what is going on. He tells her that people are celebrating a religious festival. It is all very colourful. They go down to the river to eat their picnic. Wendy has a big piece of pork pie and Sam and Gus eat the ham sandwiches. They cross the bridge and get on the London Eye. As they reach the top they can see all of London. The Houses of Parliament look tiny! Wendy tells Sam that this has been the best excursion she has ever had. Sam takes this as a great compliment.

16b Reading Comprehension

Answer the following questions on a separate sheet of paper.

1. What two words does the story use to describe Wendy's personality?
2. What is going on outside the Houses of Parliament?
3. Who does Wendy ask about what is going on?
4. What does Wendy tell Sam?
5. How does Sam feel about what Wendy tells him?

16c Wordsearch

There are 8 words from the story hidden in the box below. They go from left to right and top to bottom.

c	m	a	g	n	i	f	i	c	e	n	t
o	f	h	t	x	a	g	k	y	v	m	o
h	a	n	d	k	e	r	c	h	i	e	f
f	g	d	s	g	u	l	o	s	x	b	o
s	e	t	v	h	t	d	n	o	p	a	b
b	e	l	i	e	v	e	f	g	r	a	e
i	o	n	c	d	e	x	u	s	i	c	d
s	v	g	d	s	v	j	s	u	e	d	i
f	n	i	e	c	e	j	i	k	s	v	e
r	t	y	b	d	a	e	o	m	t	w	n
x	s	e	g	z	v	h	n	m	k	l	c
p	r	o	c	e	s	s	i	o	n	z	e

16d New Words

On a separate sheet of paper, write down 6 words from the 'sion', 'ie/ei' and 'ent/ence' word families. Try to think of 2 words for each family.

16e Drawing

On a separate sheet of paper draw a picture of the Houses of Parliament and colour it in.

17. Various   **Spelling Made Easy**
     'al', 'y' (i), 'ea' (ē)   **Level 3 Textbook**
                                                           Pages 58 – 63

17a Reading Exercise

The Carnival: Part One

Every year, people from Sam's village go to the nearest city to take part in the annual carnival. It is lots of fun. There is a choral performance in the cathedral, a folk festival and colourful musical events. This year Sam is taking part. He is playing the cymbal in the local village band. They will play one song as part of the evening concert. Sam is very excited. He has not performed since the Christmas concert the previous year, and he really enjoyed that. Gus is also in the band. He is playing his flute. It is a fun way to apply their talents and occupy their time.

The morning of the carnival arrives. The weather is beautiful and sunny. Sam and Gus decide to cycle to the city. They get up early so that they can ride in peace without having to put up with bad traffic. Gus rides his tricycle and Sam takes his bent, blue bike. The ride takes around an hour and a half. Gus has to stop once to grease his brakes, but this doesn't really hold them up. Sam is usually very punctual, and they time the journey perfectly. They arrive at the central square of the city at exactly half past ten. They unload their instruments from their cycle baskets and get ready to have some fun. They hope nothing will go awry!

17b Reading Comprehension

Answer the following questions on a separate sheet of paper.

1. Where does the choral performance take place?
2. What two reasons does the story give for Sam and Gus's involvement in the carnival?
3. Why do Sam and Gus get up early?
4. What does Gus stop to do on the journey?
5. What word from the story means 'to be on time'?

17c Wordsearch

There are 8 words from the story hidden in the box below. They go from left to right and top to bottom.

b	a	n	n	u	a	l	g	h	t
e	w	r	c	e	n	t	r	a	l
v	r	b	s	w	y	u	e	x	b
u	y	n	a	x	s	c	a	h	j
g	b	c	p	p	x	y	s	e	z
w	q	u	p	o	v	c	e	z	n
f	g	n	l	h	j	l	k	x	m
t	o	m	y	c	p	e	a	c	e
v	b	n	h	o	h	z	w	q	m
c	a	r	n	i	v	a	l	b	h

17d Find the Word

Take a red pen and carefully circle all the words in the story that are from the 'al', 'y' and 'ea' word families.

17e Creative Writing

On a separate sheet of paper write a paragraph of 100 words about your favourite band.

18 Various
   'al', 'y' (i), 'ea' (ē)

Spelling Made Easy
Level 3 Textbook
Pages 58 – 63

18a Reading Exercise

The Carnival: Part Two

Sam and Gus park their bikes. They are both hungry after the long ride into the city. There are lots of food stalls set up for the carnival. The two friends decide to treat themselves as a reward for the exercise they have taken. Sam buys himself a big greasy hotdog and Gus has an enormous slab of treacle tart. They both gulp down a beaker of cider too. They feel full and satisfied. They have the rest of the day to enjoy the carnival before they have to play in the evening concert.

They start to wander around. The city is full of amazing things. You can pay £5 to have your picture taken holding an eagle, and £10 to hold a real python. Gus does not like snakes so he moves swiftly away! Sam wants to watch the professional acrobats who are doing a display. He can't believe how fearless they are! Gus meets some friends and stops for a chat. The carnival is always a very social event. At last it is time for the evening concert to begin. Sam and Gus take their places in the village band. Gus has a solo in the piece they are playing. No-one can deny that he is a rather musical chap and gets a clap all to himself. Sam has to hit the cymbal once right at the end of the piece. This is his favourite moment and he gets it just right. He hits the cymbal right in the centre and grins from ear to ear as the crowd lets out a cheer.

18b Reading Comprehension

Answer the following questions on a separate sheet of paper.

1. What do Sam and Gus buy to eat and drink?
2. What can you do for £5 at the carnival?
3. What can you do for £10 at the carnival?
4. Why does Gus get a clap all to himself?
5. What does Sam play in the band?

18c Wordsearch

There are 8 words from the story hidden in the box below. They go from left to right and top to bottom.

t	c	a	r	n	i	v	a	l	u	c	o
f	g	j	k	l	e	r	x	z	o	y	u
f	d	x	z	g	b	k	f	x	m	m	o
r	e	t	t	r	e	a	c	l	e	b	n
w	n	q	s	e	f	y	u	c	n	a	m
y	y	c	x	a	z	g	j	u	f	l	m
t	h	k	c	s	z	u	j	l	c	z	b
c	x	z	p	y	t	h	o	n	y	t	h
g	h	j	k	c	s	t	i	e	l	s	n
p	r	o	f	e	s	s	i	o	n	a	l
y	u	c	d	g	f	s	a	p	j	b	f
d	f	b	e	a	k	e	r	n	m	d	z

18d New Words

On a separate sheet of paper, write down 8 words from the 'sion', 'al', 'y' and 'ea' word families. Try to think of 2 words for each family.

18e Drawing

On a separate sheet of paper draw a picture of Gus playing his flute and Sam playing the cymbal and colour it in.

19. Various
'our', 'ance/ant'

Spelling Made Easy
Level 3 Textbook
Pages 64 – 67

19a Reading Exercise

Strange Disappearances: Part One

Sam has heard an odd rumour going around his neighbourhood. It seems that things have been going missing from people's houses and gardens. There are never any signs of a break-in or damage, and the missing items are not really valuable. The strangest thing of all is that a couple of weeks later, the missing things turn up somewhere in the village – maybe in a bush or down a ditch. Sam's next door neighbour had a tambourine stolen that she later found underneath her car. Sam's sister had her daughter's toy elephant taken. She found it after three days up a tree in the garden. Everyone can see the humour in the situation, but it is still all very mysterious and a bit of a nuisance!

Sam and Gus decide to investigate the problem. Gus has an old acquaintance who is a retired detective. Gus thinks he might be able to help. Gus's friend needs no encouragement. He loves a good mystery to solve! His name is Gilbert and he is a very elegant man. Gilbert arrives the very next morning and sets up his detecting equipment in Sam's house. He tells Sam and Gus that he will need some assistance. Sam and Gus readily volunteer themselves. Gilbert says they must watch the entrance of the house opposite to try and catch the strange thief. Sam and Gus nod their heads earnestly. It is very exciting, but they will need courage.

19b Reading Comprehension

Answer the following questions on a separate sheet of paper.

1. What is going around Sam's neighbourhood?
2. What did Sam's next door neighbour have stolen?
3. What did the daughter of Sam's sister have stolen?
4. What word is used in the story to describe Gilbert?
5. What does Gilbert tell Sam and Gus to watch as part of the investigation?

19c Wordsearch

There are 8 words from the story hidden in the box below. They go from left to right and top to bottom.

f	g	h	s	c	h	y	u	e	i	p	u
e	l	e	p	h	a	n	t	l	h	m	c
j	u	y	x	b	s	z	q	e	w	r	t
g	h	j	n	c	s	p	a	g	r	t	x
a	c	q	u	a	i	n	t	a	n	c	e
f	g	h	x	z	s	t	u	n	p	o	m
w	q	z	v	h	t	a	e	t	n	u	o
x	f	a	l	p	a	c	s	t	u	r	b
n	u	i	s	a	n	c	e	b	n	a	x
d	f	g	y	u	c	m	v	x	s	g	a
f	t	y	c	j	e	a	l	k	m	e	w
h	u	m	o	u	r	r	u	m	o	u	r

19d Find the Word

Take a red pen and carefully circle all the words in the story that are from the 'our' and 'ance/ant' word families.

19e Creative Writing

On a separate sheet of paper write a paragraph of 100 words about your favourite toy or game.

20. Various
  'our', 'ance/ant'

Spelling Made Easy
Level 3 Textbook
Pages 64 – 67

20a Reading Exercise

Strange Disappearances: Part Two

Sam, Gus and Gilbert are trying to solve the mystery of the disappearing items. They are observing the front entrance of the house opposite Sam's. The front door of the house is some distance away, so they need to use a telescope to see it properly. Gilbert says they must work under cover of night and wear dark colours. Sam thinks Gilbert's behaviour is a little extravagant, but Gus assures him that Gilbert always gets results. Sam admits that he is ignorant of the ways of the professional detective, so he keeps quiet.

That night Sam, Gus and Gilbert lie in the grass in Sam's front garden just waiting and watching. Suddenly, there is a rustle in the bushes. Sam and Gus clutch each other, scared. What if it is an angry burglar? Will he find them? Sam looks at Gilbert. The retired detective seems very calm. He is almost smiling. His behaviour is reassuring to the nervous pair of friends. Just then, a huge cat runs across the road and gracefully leaps through the open window of the house over the road. The cat stays inside the house for a moment, and then reappears at the window with a little wooden bird in its mouth. It jumps down from the sill and runs away into the night. Gilbert leaps up and claps his hands. The mystery is solved, and Sam and Gus can finally put an end to the rumour of the strange disappearances!

20b Reading Comprehension

Answer the following questions on a separate sheet of paper.

1. How far away from Sam and Gus is the front door of the house opposite?
2. What does Gilbert say Sam and Gus must wear?
3. What does Sam think of Gilbert's behaviour?
4. Why does he keep quiet about his opinion of Gilbert?
5. What can Sam and Gus finally put an end to, as a result of their investigation?

20c Wordsearch

There are 6 words from the story hidden in the box below. They go from left to right and top to bottom.

e	n	t	r	a	n	c	e	h	j
d	t	h	x	s	m	p	g	x	w
g	c	o	l	o	u	r	s	z	h
g	d	i	s	t	a	n	c	e	m
j	k	l	p	h	c	d	c	r	b
i	g	n	o	r	a	n	t	u	n
f	g	y	h	b	z	s	q	m	a
p	o	h	v	c	x	d	h	o	m
g	b	e	h	a	v	i	o	u	r
b	h	d	s	e	q	w	p	r	x

20d New Words

On a separate sheet of paper, write down 6 words from the 'our' and 'ance/ant' word families. Try to think of 3 words for each family.

20e Drawing

On a separate sheet of paper draw a picture of a cat with a wooden bird in its mouth then colour it in.

ANSWERS (pages 2-3)

1. Magic 'e'
   'a-e', 'i-e', 'o-e', 'u-e'

**Spelling Made Easy
Level 3 Textbook
Pages 6 – 13**

1b Reading Comprehension

Correct answers are likely to include the following key words or sentences.

1. **Like company, love to laugh, adventures.**
2. **Hot chocolate with whipped cream.**
3. **Noisy cat.**
4. **Advertisement for dilapidated house.**
5. **Repair, make safe, hotel.**

1c Wordsearch

c	h	o	c	o	l	a	t	e	p
x	r	a	u	m	a	h	r	d	e
s	v	c	w	t	g	o	s	b	r
c	g	q	u	n	u	z	u	x	s
o	m	u	f	s	a	r	r	y	u
n	l	i	k	e	l	y	e	j	a
e	k	r	i	f	d	b	r	w	d
a	v	e	r	b	p	l	a	c	e
x	d	i	s	u	s	e	d	w	b
n	i	n	e	t	e	e	n	a	v

1d Find the Word

Sam and Gus have been great friends for many years. They **like** one another's company, they love to laugh and they have had many **adventures** together. One **fine** morning, Sam and Gus are sitting in a café. Sam is having a cup of coffee, and Gus is having his favourite drink – a large mug of hot **chocolate** with whipped cream. They each have a **scone** and jam to eat. They are reading **separate** newspapers and chatting happily. Sam is feeling a little **tired** because a noisy cat has kept him up all night. He yawns **widely** and **takes** a sip of his tea.
Suddenly, Gus sits up very straight. He seems **excited** about something he has seen in his paper. He shows Sam an **advertisement** on **page nineteen**. It gives details of an old, **dilapidated** house that is for **sale**. Gus wants to **acquire** the house and repair it, **make** it **safe** and turn it into a top **hotel**. He thinks it would be fun, and they could **make** a lot of money and **retire**! Sam is not so **sure**. He wants to **take** a good look at the house to see the damage. It has been **disused** for over twenty years and is **likely** to be beyond repair. They **decide** to go to the house immediately. Gus believes that he can **definitely persuade** Sam to buy the **place** . . .

ANSWERS (pages 4-5)

2. Magic 'e'
   'a-e', 'i-e', 'o-e', 'u-e'

Spelling Made Easy
Level 3 Textbook
Pages 6 – 13

2b Reading Comprehension

Correct answers are likely to include the following key words or sentences.

1. **Dilapidated, dark, dirty, rises high, loneliness, eroded.**
2. **Strange feeling.**
3. **Accommodate, hotel.**
4. **To leave / made a mistake.**
5. **Gates.**

2c Wordsearch

a	c	c	o	m	m	o	d	a	t	e
d	g	d	u	n	z	s	x	d	e	c
g	r	f	d	s	w	t	h	m	m	u
m	i	s	t	a	k	e	g	i	p	z
w	s	i	f	h	y	f	r	r	e	n
t	e	c	v	o	a	v	b	e	r	p
c	v	b	r	a	v	e	l	y	a	r
p	i	c	t	u	r	e	w	c	t	o
b	v	e	y	s	s	v	y	b	u	b
f	s	l	o	p	e	y	a	v	r	e
w	q	d	e	f	i	n	i	t	e	z

ANSWERS (pages 6-7)

3. Various
Double Consonants 1, 'ur', 'tion'

Spelling Made Easy
Level 3 Textbook
Pages 14 – 19

3b Reading Comprehension

Correct answers are likely to include the following key words or sentences.

1. **Suburbs.**
2. **Directions.**
3. **Address.**
4. **Pursue.**
5. **Urgency, instincts, courage of conviction.**

3c Wordsearch

d	**i**	**r**	**e**	**c**	**t**	**i**	**o**	**n**	**d**
a	g	h	s	e	s	v	p	j	**i**
s	u	**m**	**e**	**n**	**t**	**i**	**o**	**n**	**s**
t	**p**	**u**	**r**	**s**	**u**	**e**	g	k	a
a	z	w	t	f	r	h	i	l	**p**
t	v	o	s	c	**g**	f	g	s	**p**
i	**a**	**d**	**d**	**r**	**e**	**s**	**s**	a	**e**
o	g	h	d	u	**n**	b	w	m	**a**
n	t	y	c	s	**c**	n	m	t	**r**
r	**f**	**o**	**g**	**g**	**y**	h	d	a	**s**

3d Find the Word

It is a cold and **foggy** night. A couple called Adam and Cherry have sent Sam and Gus an **invitation** to come for **dinner**, and now the pair of friends are on their way to Adam and Cherry's home in the sleepy **suburbs** of London. Adam and Cherry sent Sam an email with **directions** to the house, but Sam has left the printout at home, and now he and Gus are lost. Sam can just remember the **address**, and he and Gus are walking around the area, trying to find a person to ask for help. A man creeps out of a bush by the side of the road, making Gus jump. The man had been **hidden** by the fog. Gus calls out to him, but he just looks round and then **disappears** into the night.
Sam is **disappointed**, but Gus has a strange feeling about the man. He paid close **attention** to the man's face and clothes. He **mentions** his odd feeling to Sam, and thinks they should **pursue** the man. Sam knows that they are late for Adam and Cherry, but he hears the **urgency** in his friend's voice. Gus has good instincts and a courage of **conviction** about his feelings, so Sam agrees to go after the man. They move quickly and quietly in the **direction** the strange man took. He seems to have headed back towards the **station** so the two excited friends retrace their steps.

ANSWERS (pages 8-9)

4. Various
Double Consonants 1, 'ur', 'tion'

Spelling Made Easy
Level 3 Textbook
Pages 14 – 19

4b Reading Comprehension

Correct answers are likely to include the following key words or sentences.

1. **Spate of burglaries, gang lurking.**
2. **Broken glass.**
3. **Surprise the burglar in action.**
4. **Dagger.**
5. **Interruption.**

4c Wordsearch

h	**a**	**p**	**p**	**e**	**n**	**i**	**n**	**g**	d
a	**d**	**i**	**r**	**e**	**c**	**t**	**i**	**o**	**n**
f	g	s	r	u	d	s	t	m	w
o	**b**	**u**	**r**	**g**	**l**	**a**	**r**	f	a
j	d	e	y	h	u	k	p	o	c
d	**a**	**g**	**g**	**e**	**r**	j	l	g	t
c	f	v	b	n	k	t	y	g	i
s	**u**	**r**	**p**	**r**	**i**	**s**	**e**	y	o
w	q	f	t	g	n	g	m	b	n
f	g	s	r	y	**g**	**l**	**a**	**s**	**s**

ANSWERS (pages 10-11)

5. Various
Soft c, Double Consonants 2, . . . ful

Spelling Made Easy
Level 3 Textbook
Pages 20 – 25

5b Reading Comprehension

Correct answers are likely to include the following key words or sentences.

1. **Circus.**
2. **Clowns.**
3. **Wonderful.**
4. **Terrible, accident in tunnel.**
5. **Skilful.**

5c Wordsearch

g	h	r	u	n	n	i	n	g	u	f
a	c	c	e	l	e	r	a	t	o	r
n	e	g	s	v	s	e	a	r	b	m
n	s	w	c	r	t	c	v	g	h	k
o	k	j	i	d	s	o	t	s	q	o
y	i	b	r	i	l	l	i	a	n	t
e	l	g	c	b	x	l	w	q	i	m
d	f	i	u	q	w	e	b	f	x	o
s	u	v	s	b	u	c	y	o	e	i
z	l	f	g	s	r	t	i	f	o	f
a	w	o	n	d	e	r	f	u	l	g

5d Find the Word

It is a **beautiful** sunny morning. Sam wakes up very **excited**. He is going on a trip to the **circus**. Sam loves the **circus**. He thinks it is **brilliant**. He **really** loves the clowns when they throw buckets of water over each other. Even when he is **annoyed** about something, he will **recollect** the time he saw clowns when he was a young boy and have a good laugh. Sam's best friend Gus is going to the **circus** too. He also thinks clowns are **wonderful**! Sam has his breakfast and gets **dressed**. He drives to Gus's **little** house and beeps the horn. Gus runs out and climbs into the **passenger** seat. Sam puts his foot on the **accelerator** and they are on their way!
The **circus** starts at three o'clock. It is already half past two and they are **running** late. They get to the **tunnel** that runs under the river. The **traffic** is **terrible**. There has been an **accident** inside the **tunnel**. Sam is a **skilful** driver, but there is nothing he can do. They are stuck. Sam puts the radio on **nice** and loud. Gus's favourite song is playing and they both sing along. The people in the other cars see that Sam and Gus are having a good time, and they put their own radios on. The sun is shining and it is a lovely day. Sam and Gus are late for the **circus** but they are not too **annoyed**. They will make it in time to see the clowns.

ANSWERS (pages 12-13)

6. **Various**
    Soft c, Double Consonants 2, . . . ful

    Spelling Made Easy
    Level 3 Textbook
    Pages 20 – 25

6b Reading Comprehension

Correct answers are likely to include the following key words or sentences.

1. **Not bitter, accept, grateful for radio.**
2. **Accident.**
3. **Red and yellow.**
4. **Beautiful.**
5. **Run into the wrong entrance.**

6c Wordsearch

d	**h**	**o**	**p**	**e**	**f**	**u**	**l**	**a**	w
v	b	a	**b**	f	d	s	n	**c**	m
h	j	i	**i**	g	h	m	k	**c**	**s**
g	**r**	**a**	**t**	**e**	**f**	**u**	**l**	e	**p**
f	t	n	**t**	a	s	d	k	**s**	a
e	r	t	**e**	s	c	a	h	**s**	**c**
a	**g**	**g**	**r**	**e**	**s**	**s**	**i**	**v**	**e**
f	a	y	b	n	u	j	f	k	l
z	**t**	**r**	**a**	**f**	**f**	**i**	**c**	x	c
w	t	y	x	**a**	**c**	**c**	**e**	**p**	**t**

ANSWERS (pages 14-15)

7. Various
'ch' (k), 'ly', 'or'

Spelling Made Easy
Level 3 Textbook
Pages 26 – 31

7b Reading Comprehension

Correct answers are likely to include the following key words or sentences.

1. **Decorations, Christmas.**
2. **Christmas choir.**
3. **Never been involved in a performance.**
4. **Gus is no ordinary man.**
5. **School.**

7c Wordsearch

w	**a**	f	c	z	a	g	j	u	**o**
x	**s**	**c**	**h**	**o**	**o**	**l**	o	**s**	**r**
v	**s**	b	u	i	d	s	t	**t**	**d**
i	**o**	v	**c**	**h**	**o**	**i**	**r**	**o**	**i**
d	**r**	v	f	s	a	t	h	**m**	**n**
o	**t**	a	s	c	g	d	p	**a**	**a**
d	**e**	**c**	**o**	**r**	**a**	**t**	e	**c**	**r**
g	**d**	w	h	k	o	p	m	h	**y**
f	g	r	e	a	**l**	**l**	**y**	j	i
c	**h**	**r**	**i**	**s**	**t**	**m**	**a**	**s**	l

7d Find the Word

It is **Christmas** and Sam wants to **decorate** his house. Gus comes over to help out. Sam gets a box of **assorted decorations** down from the attic and the two friends begin **immediately**. It takes around three hours but when they have finished they feel **really** pleased with their work. They have **decorated** the house **beautifully**. Now it's **really** starting to feel like **Christmas**!
Gus shows Sam a clipping from the local newspaper. It is for a **Christmas choir** at the local **school** hall. Anybody can join, no matter how musical they are. There will be one rehearsal and then there will be a concert in the evening. It sounds very exciting! Sam and Gus decide to go along and join in. Sam is **particularly** looking **forward** to the concert as he has never been involved in a big **performance before**. Gus is excited too, but he is also very nervous about singing in public. He feels a knot in his **stomach**. Gus is a brave man and he does not like feeling nervous about things. He wants to confront his nerves and **really** get stuck in! Gus is no **ordinary** man and that is why Sam likes him so much. They change their clothes – they need to be smart **for** the **performance**. Gus and Sam have a last look at the **beautifully decorated** house and head off to the **school**.

ANSWERS (pages 16-17)

8. Various
'ch' (k), 'ly', 'or'

Spelling Made Easy
Level 3 Textbook
Pages 26 – 31

8b Reading Comprehension

Correct answers are likely to include the following key words or sentences.

1. **Couple called Christine and Christopher.**
2. **Make people quiet to organise the rehearsal.**
3. **Orchestra.**
4. **Mayor; junior and senior members of the local community.**
5. **Organ sounds a chord.**

8c Wordsearch

s	p	o	n	s	o	r	e	g	j
o	d	f	r	a	e	f	c	u	o
r	h	k	l	s	t	x	h	b	r
g	t	y	s	a	j	k	o	n	c
a	m	o	r	g	a	n	g	w	h
n	d	s	r	y	s	b	j	d	e
i	u	q	u	i	e	t	l	y	s
s	f	g	s	r	a	z	y	w	t
e	m	k	d	c	h	o	r	d	r
e	x	c	i	t	e	d	l	y	a

ANSWERS (pages 18-19)

9. Various
Silent Letters 1 and 2, 'ough/eigh'

Spelling Made Easy
Level 3 Textbook
Pages 32 – 37

9b   Reading Comprehension

Correct answers are likely to include the following key words or sentences.

1. **Building work.**
2. **Eight.**
3. **Knot.**
4. **Scientific.**
5. **Neighbour.**

9c   Wordsearch

w	b	u	i	l	d	i	n	g	e
r	t	y	x	b	g	h	a	u	s
s	c	i	e	n	t	i	f	i	c
r	t	y	v	s	h	u	p	n	e
m	i	p	o	g	d	w	o	s	n
e	s	a	n	s	w	e	r	i	e
i	b	v	f	m	j	u	l	g	r
g	a	k	n	e	e	l	s	n	y
h	e	s	f	s	v	g	j	k	u
t	h	o	r	o	u	g	h	o	i

9d   Find the Word

Sam is having some **building** work done on his house and garden to improve the **scenery**. He goes into the garden to gather up his collection of **gnomes**. Sam has a great collection of **gnomes** and he loves them all. There **ought** to be **eight gnomes**, but today, Sam can only count seven. One of his **gnomes** is missing! Sam cannot think what has happened. He calls his best friend Gus. Gus does not **know** either. He can give Sam no **answer**. Sam is upset. He makes a **thorough** search of the garden, trying to find his **eighth gnome**. He **kneels** down and looks in all the nooks and crannies. He feels a **knot** in his stomach as he realises that the **gnome** is missing.
Sam feels awful so he asks Gus to come over. Gus arrives with a **sign** he has found on his way over. It says, '**SCIENTIFIC** EXPERIMENT! I can make your garden **gnomes** come to life! Bring me the **gnomes** and I will show you how . . . Professor Alan Fluggle, 3a Windmill Lane.' Sam realises with a jolt that Professor Alan Fluggle is his **neighbour**. Gus tells Sam that he has had a brilliant idea. He thinks they should take one of Sam's remaining **gnomes** to Professor Fluggle, and when he comes to life Sam can ask him what happened to the missing **gnome**. Sam listens to Gus's idea. **Although** he feels it is a little odd, he cannot see what else to do. Sam chooses a clever looking **gnome** and they set off.

ANSWERS (pages 20-21)

10. Various
Silent Letters 1 and 2, 'ough/eigh'

Spelling Made Easy
Level 3 Textbook
Pages 32 – 37

10b Reading Comprehension

Correct answers are likely to include the following key words or sentences.

1. **Professor Alan Fluggle, Mad Scientist and Gnome Lover.**
2. **Gnarled, old.**
3. **Unfastens.**
4. **Guilty.**
5. **Biscuit.**

10c Wordsearch

w	r	**c**	**o**	**u**	**g**	**h**	**s**	o	**g**
d	f	g	t	y	u	c	z	s	**n**
f	j	o	r	v	s	a	w	m	**o**
k	**n**	**o**	**c**	**k**	**e**	**r**	**o**	w	**m**
e	t	u	b	s	g	z	**u**	t	**e**
w	n	**s**	**c**	**e**	**n**	**e**	**g**	a	d
r	f	h	y	u	s	n	**h**	m	l
e	**b**	**i**	**s**	**c**	**u**	**i**	**t**	w	t
c	c	v	b	s	q	f	k	l	g
k	j	k	**g**	**u**	**i**	**l**	**t**	**y**	u

ANSWERS (pages 22-23)

11. Various
'Soft g', 'ar', 'ous', 'ary/able'

Spelling Made Easy
Level 3 Textbook
Pages 38 – 45

11b Reading Comprehension

Correct answers are likely to include the following key words or sentences.

1. **Fruit and vegetables.**
2. **Apple orchard.**
3. **Damage.**
4. **Extra custard.**
5. **Nervous, awkward.**

11c Wordsearch

v	e	g	e	t	a	b	l	e	s
o	f	f	g	t	y	u	n	m	f
c	d	a	n	e	r	v	o	u	s
a	a	m	g	y	m	h	j	k	d
r	m	o	h	u	p	c	z	s	w
d	a	u	r	t	c	n	z	x	f
i	g	s	f	o	r	w	a	r	d
g	e	g	j	i	p	v	z	s	w
a	m	n	c	d	j	u	s	w	a
n	e	c	e	s	s	a	r	y	o

11d Find the Word

Sam is **famous** throughout his village for his terrible eating habits. He eats lots of fatty foods because he thinks they taste good. He also does very little exercise. As a result Sam is very unfit. His friend Gus is the exact opposite. Gus loves to eat fruit and **vegetables** and he goes to the **gym** three times a week. Gus always has lots of **energy**. He loves to work in his **garden**. He has an apple **orchard** at the back of his **garden** and he picks the apples off the trees and eats them. Gus is very **knowledgeable** about healthy food and getting fit. Gus believes Sam is doing himself some **damage** by eating so badly.
One day, Sam and Gus are having lunch in Sam's favourite restaurant. Sam leans **forward** to eat a plate of chips and one of the buttons on his **cardigan** pops off. It hits an old lady in the face, which **startles** her. Sam ignores the button and orders a bowl of crumble with extra **custard** for pudding. Gus does not order any pudding. Sam licks his bowl clean and does a big burp. Sam's belly looks huge. Gus frowns – he feels the time is right to tell Sam that he is concerned about his lifestyle. He thinks a change is **necessary**. It could be **awkward**, so Gus knows he must be sensitive. Gus feels a bit **nervous** as he doesn't want to get into an argument with Sam.

ANSWERS (pages 24-25)

12. Various
**   'Soft g', 'ar', 'ous', 'ary/able'**

Spelling Made Easy
Level 3 Textbook
Pages 38 – 45

12b Reading Comprehension

Correct answers are likely to include the following key words or sentences.

1. **Fit into trousers he wore as a young man.**
2. **January.**
3. **Vegetables.**
4. **Marmalade and margarine.**
5. **New cardigan.**

12c Wordsearch

d	e	p	a	r	t	m	e	n	t
o	h	a	r	d	f	a	h	d	z
w	r	t	y	v	x	n	o	p	a
b	h	g	t	z	w	a	m	k	z
j	u	k	i	m	a	g	i	n	e
w	g	b	h	j	l	e	m	w	z
f	e	b	r	u	a	r	y	o	p
d	g	u	b	z	v	f	o	i	z
d	t	s	p	a	c	i	o	u	s
m	a	r	g	a	r	i	n	e	m

ANSWERS (pages 26-27)

13. Various
'le', 'er', 'y' (i)

Spelling Made Easy
Level 3 Textbook
Pages 46 – 51

13b Reading Comprehension

Correct answers are likely to include the following key words or sentences.

1. **Cold, rainy, bad, generally miserable.**
2. **Italy/Mediterranean.**
3. **Egypt.**
4. **Get into pyjamas, wait in bedrooms.**
5. **Mysterious crypts.**

13c Wordsearch

p	y	p	y	r	a	m	i	d	s
y	g	h	s	e	y	v	u	e	p
j	a	c	r	y	p	t	y	s	u
a	b	m	w	e	t	z	g	p	n
m	i	s	e	r	a	b	l	e	c
a	y	u	c	s	g	j	s	r	l
s	p	i	c	s	z	s	a	a	e
y	d	e	s	e	r	t	j	t	z
x	f	t	b	k	s	w	d	e	l
i	n	c	r	e	d	i	b	l	e

13d Find the Word

Sam and Gus are fed up with the bad weather in the village. It is cold, **rainy** and **generally miserable**. Sam is **desperate** to see some sunshine. He and his friend Gus decide to go on holiday. They log on to the **internet** to find a last minute deal. Gus loves the **Mediterranean** and wants to go to **Italy**, but Sam finds a cheap holiday to **Egypt**. Neither Sam nor Gus has ever been to Africa, but Sam's **uncle** has. Sam manages to **persuade** Gus to take the deal to **Egypt**. They enter their credit card details, click the button and the holiday is booked. In less than a week, they will be on an aeroplane to **Egypt** and sunny **weather**. It is all very exciting!
It is the night before the holiday. Sam and Gus have to get up very early next morning to catch the plane. Gus stays **over** at Sam's house. They both get into their **pyjamas** at half past eight and sit in their separate bedrooms waiting. They are too excited to sleep. Sam is thinking about the **Pyramids**. He knows they will be **incredible** and he cannot wait to see them. Gus is dreaming about **mysterious crypts** that he can explore. They both hope that the **temperature** will be high. They drift into a light sleep and dream of the old Kings and Queens of **Egypt**, the sandy **desert** and camel rides. Suddenly the alarm clock goes off. Sam and Gus jump up and throw on their travelling clothes. They grab their suitcases, jump into Sam's car and head to the airport.

ANSWERS (pages 28-29)

14. Various
'le', 'er', 'y' (i)

Spelling Made Easy
Level 3 Textbook
Pages 46 – 51

14b   Reading Comprehension

Correct answers are likely to include the following key words or sentences.

1. **Thermometer.**
2. **Drawers.**
3. **Monastery.**
4. **Pyramids.**
5. **Pebble.**

14c   Wordsearch

h	f	h	t	j	c	a	e	y	j	l
o	i	m	p	o	s	s	i	b	l	e
r	b	n	d	r	s	a	e	y	j	k
r	x	m	y	s	t	e	r	y	c	f
i	v	j	l	u	i	t	v	d	l	i
b	o	s	c	r	a	m	b	l	e	e
l	f	d	r	s	g	n	m	c	s	r
e	r	y	y	j	k	d	q	o	p	y
t	e	m	p	e	r	a	t	u	r	e
b	v	z	t	w	e	g	y	k	g	d
m	o	n	a	s	t	e	r	y	a	f

55

ANSWERS (pages 30-31)

15. Various
'sion', 'ie/ei', 'ent/ence'

Spelling Made Easy
Level 3 Textbook
Pages 52 – 57

15b Reading Comprehension

Correct answers are likely to include the following key words or sentences.

1. **Interesting announcement.**
2. **Niece.**
3. **Permission.**
4. **Sense of occasion.**
5. **Lets out a piercing shriek.**

15c Wordsearch

i	l	o	c	c	a	s	i	o	n	h
n	g	d	s	h	r	i	e	k	a	d
t	r	e	s	i	d	e	n	t	s	i
e	e	g	j	k	l	n	x	z	a	l
l	c	e	d	e	c	i	s	i	o	n
l	e	f	b	m	s	e	w	t	s	z
i	i	b	h	k	d	c	t	y	z	w
g	v	e	w	q	z	e	b	k	c	z
e	e	m	l	k	v	u	o	f	g	p
n	s	e	x	c	u	r	s	i	o	n
t	r	t	z	a	m	p	w	q	r	u

15d Find the Word

Sam is watching **television** when he sees an interesting **announcement**. There is an invitation to all the **residents** of his village to visit the Houses of **Parliament**. Sam thinks he would like an **excursion** to London and so he calls up his best **friend** Gus. Gus has seen the **announcement** too, and thinks it is a great idea. Sam would like to invite his **niece** Wendy. She is ten years old and has never been to London or the Houses of **Parliament** before. Wendy asks her mother for **permission** to go. She **receives permission** and they make a **decision** to go the very next day.
The next morning Sam, Gus and Sam's **niece** Wendy meet at nine o'clock to catch the train to London. Wendy is a very **intelligent** and **obedient** girl, and so Sam knows they will all have a great day. To give a sense of **occasion**, Wendy's mother has packed a very expensive picnic, using the very best **ingredients** money can buy. They are all looking forward to eating it at lunchtime! The train is about to arrive at King's Cross station. Wendy lets out a **piercing shriek** of **excitement**. She cannot wait to get off the train. She is looking forward to seeing the green benches in the House of Commons and the red benches in the House of Lords. She is also excited about going on the London Eye and being high above the capital city. It will be a great **experience**.

ANSWERS (pages 32-33)

16. Various
'sion', 'ie/ei', 'ent/ence'

Spelling Made Easy
Level 3 Textbook
Pages 52 – 57

16b Reading Comprehension

Correct answers are likely to include the following key words or sentences.

1. **Intelligence/obedience.**
2. **Procession.**
3. **Priest.**
4. **Best excursion ever.**
5. **Great compliment.**

16c Wordsearch

c	**m**	**a**	**g**	**n**	**i**	**f**	**i**	**c**	**e**	**n**	**t**
o	f	h	t	x	a	g	k	y	v	m	o
h	**a**	**n**	**d**	**k**	**e**	**r**	**c**	**h**	**i**	**e**	**f**
f	g	d	s	g	u	l	o	s	x	b	o
s	e	t	v	h	t	d	n	o	p	a	b
b	**e**	**l**	**i**	**e**	**v**	**e**	f	g	r	a	e
i	o	n	c	d	e	x	u	s	i	c	d
s	v	g	d	s	v	j	s	u	e	d	i
f	**n**	**i**	**e**	**c**	**e**	j	i	k	s	v	e
r	t	y	b	d	a	e	o	m	t	w	n
x	s	e	g	z	v	h	n	m	k	l	c
p	**r**	**o**	**c**	**e**	**s**	**s**	**i**	**o**	**n**	z	e

ANSWERS (pages 34-35)

17. Various
'al', 'y' (i), 'ea' (ē)

Spelling Made Easy
Level 3 Textbook
Pages 58 – 63

17b Reading Comprehension

Correct answers are likely to include the following key words or sentences.

1. **Cathedral.**
2. **Apply their talents; occupy their time.**
3. **Ride in peace, no bad traffic.**
4. **Grease his brakes.**
5. **Punctual.**

17c Wordsearch

b	**a**	**n**	**n**	**u**	**a**	**l**	g	t
e	**w**	r	**c**	**e**	**n**	**t**	**r**	**a**	**l**
v	**r**	b	s	w	y	u	**e**	x	b
u	**y**	n	a	x	s	**c**	**a**	**h**	j
g	b	c	**p**	p	x	**y**	**s**	e	z
w	q	u	**p**	o	v	**c**	**e**	z	n
f	g	n	**l**	h	j	**l**	k	x	m
t	o	m	**y**	c	**p**	**e**	**a**	**c**	**e**
v	b	n	h	o	h	z	w	q	m
c	**a**	**r**	**n**	**i**	**v**	**a**	**l**	b	h

17d Find the Word

Every **year**, people from Sam's village go to the **nearest** city to take part in the **annual carnival**. It is lots of fun. There is a **choral** performance in the **cathedral**, a folk **festival** and colourful **musical** events. This year Sam is taking part. He is playing the **cymbal** in the **local** village band. They will play one song as part of the evening concert. Sam is very excited. He has not performed since the Christmas concert the previous year, and he really enjoyed that. Gus is also in the band. He is playing his flute. It is a fun way to **apply** their talents and **occupy** their time.
The morning of the **carnival** arrives. The weather is beautiful and sunny. Sam and Gus decide to **cycle** to the city. They get up early so that they can ride in **peace** without having to put up with bad traffic. Gus rides his **tricycle** and Sam takes his bent, blue bike. The ride takes around an hour and a half. Gus has to stop once to **grease** his brakes, but this doesn't really hold them up. Sam is **usually** very **punctual**, and they time the journey perfectly. They arrive at the **central** square of the city at exactly half past ten. They unload their instruments from their **cycle** baskets and get ready to have some fun. They hope nothing will go **awry**!

ANSWERS (pages 36-37)

18 Various
  'al', 'y' (i), 'ea' (ē)

Spelling Made Easy
Level 3 Textbook
Pages 58 – 63

18b Reading Comprehension

Correct answers are likely to include the following key words or sentences.

1. **Greasy hot dog, treacle tart.**
2. **Hold an eagle.**
3. **Hold a python.**
4. **He has a solo/he is musical.**
5. **Cymbal.**

18c Wordsearch

t	**c**	**a**	**r**	**i**	**v**	**a**	**l**	u	c	o
f	g	j	k	l	e	r	x	z	**y**	u
f	**d**	x	z	**g**	b	k	f	x	**m**	o
r	**e**	t	**t**	**r**	**e**	**a**	**c**	**l**	**e**	n
w	**n**	q	s	**e**	f	y	u	c	n	**a**	m
y	**y**	c	x	**a**	z	g	j	u	f	**l**	m
t	h	k	c	**s**	z	u	j	l	c	z	b
c	x	z	**p**	**y**	**t**	**h**	**o**	**n**	y	t	h
g	h	j	k	c	s	t	i	e	l	s	n
p	**r**	**o**	**f**	**e**	**s**	**s**	**i**	**o**	**n**	**a**	**l**
y	u	c	d	g	f	s	a	p	j	b	f
d	f	**b**	**e**	**a**	**k**	**e**	**r**	n	m	d	z

ANSWERS (pages 38-39)

19. Various
'our', 'ance/ant'

Spelling Made Easy
Level 3 Textbook
Pages 64 – 67

19b Reading Comprehension

Correct answers are likely to include the following key words or sentences.

1. **Odd rumour.**
2. **Tambourine.**
3. **Toy elephant.**
4. **Elegant.**
5. **Entrance of house opposite**

19c Wordsearch

f	g	h	s	c	h	y	u	e	i	p	u
e	l	e	p	h	a	n	t	l	h	m	c
j	u	y	x	b	s	z	q	e	w	r	t
g	h	j	n	c	s	p	a	g	r	t	x
a	c	q	u	a	i	n	t	a	n	c	e
f	g	h	x	z	s	t	u	n	p	o	m
w	q	z	v	h	t	a	e	t	n	u	o
x	f	a	l	p	a	c	s	t	u	r	b
n	u	i	s	a	n	c	e	b	n	a	x
d	f	g	y	u	c	m	v	x	s	g	a
f	t	y	c	j	e	a	l	k	m	e	w
h	u	m	o	u	r	r	u	m	o	u	r

19d Find the Word

Sam has heard an odd **rumour** going around his **neighbourhood**. It seems that things have been going missing from people's houses and gardens. There are never any signs of a break-in or damage, and the missing items are not really valuable. The strangest thing of all is that a couple of weeks later, the missing things turn up somewhere in the village – maybe in a bush or down a ditch. Sam's next door **neighbour** had a **tambourine** stolen that she later found underneath her car. Sam's sister had her daughter's toy **elephant** taken. She found it after three days up a tree in the garden. Everyone can see the **humour** in the situation, but it is still all very mysterious and a bit of a **nuisance**!

Sam and Gus decide to investigate the problem. Gus has an old **acquaintance** who is a retired detective. Gus thinks he might be able to help. Gus's friend needs no **encouragement**. He loves a good mystery to solve! His name is Gilbert and he is a very **elegant** man. Gilbert arrives the very next morning and sets up his detecting equipment in Sam's house. He tells Sam and Gus that he will need some **assistance**. Sam and Gus readily volunteer themselves. Gilbert says they must watch the **entrance** of the house opposite to try and catch the strange thief. Sam and Gus nod their heads earnestly. It is very exciting, but they will need **courage**.

ANSWERS (pages 40-41)

20. Various
    'our', 'ance/ant'

**Spelling Made Easy
Level 3 Textbook
Pages 64 – 67**

20b Reading Comprehension

Correct answers are likely to include the following key words or sentences.

1. **Some distance away.**
2. **Dark colours.**
3. **Extravagant**
4. **He is ignorant about professional detectives.**
5. **The rumours of strange disappearances.**

20c Wordsearch

e	n	t	r	a	n	c	e	h	j
d	t	h	x	s	m	p	g	x	w
g	c	o	l	o	u	r	s	z	h
g	d	i	s	t	a	n	c	e	m
j	k	l	p	h	c	d	c	r	b
i	g	n	o	r	a	n	t	u	n
f	g	y	h	b	z	s	q	m	a
p	o	h	v	c	x	d	h	o	m
g	b	e	h	a	v	i	o	u	r
b	h	d	s	e	q	w	p	r	x